David Hicks on home decoration

World Publishing

OTHER BOOKS BY DAVID HICKS
David Hicks on Decoration   (1966)   *Out of Print*
David Hicks on Living With Taste   (1968)   *Out of Print*
David Hicks on Bathrooms   (1970)
David Hicks on Decoration With Fabrics   (1971)

Library of Congress Catalog Card Number 72-76413.
First American Edition 1972.
First Published in Great Britain and America 1972 by
Britwell Books Limited, 43 Conduit Street, London W.1., England.
Distributed in America by World Publishing Co., New York,
New York.
Printed through Hans Blaauw with Ysel Press, Deventer, Holland.
Typesetting by Watkins Repro Service. England.

David Hicks on home decoration

To the memory of Syrie Maugham, Elsie de Wolfe, Jean-Michel Frank and Emilio Terry—four great interior decorators.

Associates

Christian Badin	Paris, France
F. Munos Cabrero	Madrid, Spain
Christopher Davis	Sydney, Australia
John Dickinson	San Francisco, U.S.A.
Philippe Garlinck	Brussels, Belgium
William Hodgins	Boston, U.S.A.
Mary Fox-Linton	London, England
Imre Loerincz	Johannesburg, S.A.
Iason Rizos	Athens, Greece
Robert Stokes	Nassau, Bahamas
Theodore Triant	New York, U.S.A.
Fleur Vulliod	Rolle, Switzerland

Acknowledgements

☐ I could not produce a book without clients who were willing to let me show my work for them in different parts of the world but as most of them prefer to remain anonymous I can only express my gratitude in general terms.

☐ Nor could I do a book without the talents of five super photographers: Michael Boys and Edward Woodman in England, Pascal Hinous and Michel Namhias in France and Norman McGrath in the United States. No less super, but merely less of their work—Julian Allason, Peter Briault, Alan Cunliffe, Kerry Dundas, Greville Photography, R. Guillemot, Elizabeth Johnston and Franchina Parisi.

☐ I should like to acknowledge the co-operation of Connaissance des Arts and Plaisir de France, and to offer my apologies to any other magazine or photographer whose loan of material has escaped me between Conduit Street and Deventer.

☐ Nick Jenkins on the strength of many small brown cigarettes has done a great job, as usual, with the layout; Andre Louw helped with clear-sighted picture editing; Mary Bailey typed and punctuated with gay precision, and my dear wife Pamela, flying between Pago Pago and Den Pasar, edited my appalling English with her unfailing patience and interest, while Guinness-Button Holdings co-ordinated with great aplomb.

☐ Since I wrote my first book on decoration, the pattern of my work has changed in that I have become involved with considerably more contract work—offices, hotels, clubs, cinemas, banks, etc. In some of the illustrations in the present book I have shown examples of my work in these areas because taste, colour, lighting, choice of furniture, use of plants and the atmosphere created thereby have many applications to the home, in the same way that the solutions for private apartments and houses have many ideas which are thoroughly applicable to contract work.

☐ In this and future books I have decided not to concentrate, as I did previously, on a specific aspect of interior decoration. I think it is more interesting to make them general and varied in their approach. For instance, in the present book, I have a group of illustrations concentrating on the use of objects, others on lighting and others on flowers, because these are important aspects of any successful interior. Whereas before I showed some illustrations from the past and the work of other designers, in this book all the rooms are ones which I have designed or decorated.

In my first book 'DAVID HICKS ON DECORATION' which was published in England in the autumn of 1966, I said many things in a rather definite, even dictatorial manner. But all the principles that I laid down then are still thoroughly applicable to the problems and solutions of 1973. And I believe that they will continue to apply in the future.

Each designer in his lifetime really has one basic breakthrough. I think I have become known for my eclectic mixture of yesterday and today, placing a Louis XVI commode in a modern room— placing a modern picture in a period room. That, combined with an overwhelming interest in lighting, in colour and in pattern, is what I feel to be my contribution to interior decoration in the latter half of the 20th Century. Any of my clients would agree that I am not a dictator, that I always try to evoke an atmosphere which they themselves can feel that they have helped to create. The purpose of this, my other and future books is to show the way in which I arrange objects, flowers, furniture—the way in which I treat a bank—the way in which I treat an office—because I believe it stimulates my readers to take another look at their problems and to create their own solutions. As I have said in another book, I do not expect anyone to copy blindly what they see illustrated in my books. I merely lay the ideas before the visually aware public in order that they may benefit from them. It isn't what you do—it's how you do it: it isn't what you possess, but how you make the most of it through the way in which you present and arrange it. ☐ In my own living room in London I have a number of different and curious objects related for me by the place where I got them, or some unusual association, but moreover related by texture, form, colour and contrast. It's the way they are placed which for me gives these relatively inexpensive objects an aesthetic value and gives the room atmosphere. As an experiment I once asked a friend to rearrange the room in my absence without deleting or adding any objects, merely changing their arrangement (this did not include the pictures or the furniture arrangement). I was delightfully surprised when I saw the result, and yet it confirmed that only I could arrange objects and possessions in a room for myself, and though the other solution (and each room has very many solutions) was pleasing, I immediately changed it back in the way that it had been before. Not that I expect the possessions and furniture of my clients to remain static—indeed, far from it. One of the most relaxing and pleasurable things in life, I think, is to rearrange one's books, one's pictures and one's smaller possessions. There is an almost never-ending series of arrangements and solutions. □ I was asked recently what changes had taken place since my first book, and although I was bound to say that I felt everything I had said in that book was still totally valid, I had also to admit that there is now a greater interest in pattern than there was then. I know this to be true, for in my product design for carpet, upholstery, curtaining, sheet and towelling manufacturers, there is an almost total concentration (apart, obviously, from a basic palette of plain colours) on pattern. It's practical, it gives atmosphere and, of course, pattern can be mixed with pattern. I believe that geometrics suit the modern lines of today's building and the streamlining of today's way of life better than plain materials and floor coverings. I have recently·

become very interested in pattern: making glazed tiles to be used in kitchens, swimming pools, bathrooms, hotel corridors; I have been designing shower curtains, ties for men, slippers, writing paper, wall-paper—all of them with definite strong, interesting patterns, varying from minute motifs to really large repeats.

☐ It is interesting to find that when I am conceiving a range of designs for menswear my previous experience in carpet designing helps me. Many of the experiments that I do in my studio with designs for clothing materials benefit my thinking in curtain design. Based firmly on tradition with one foot stuck inevitably in the past, and fascinated by the new techniques and the new fibres available, my other foot is decidedly going towards the future.

☐ A city living room and a country one need to be planned in the same way although they should produce totally different ideas. The planning of the furniture and accoutrements is the first consideration. A floorplan, however simple, is a basic necessity before attempting to arrive at a colour scheme or even a mental picture of the final look of the room as a whole. It is the manner in which we put our rooms together—the arrangements of the furniture, the lighting and hanging of pictures, the placing of objects, the style of the curtains, etc., which makes a good or poor room.

☐ It is, as always, a question of taste. Taste means selection, decision and sensitivity—if it is to be good. I have said before that I have seldom entered any room without wanting to rearrange the contents. Sometimes even perfect furniture arrangements have made my muscles itch just to alleviate the boredom of perfection by moving something to make it asymmetrical or more natural.

☐ I like all rooms to look as if they are really lived in: but above all, I believe that every room should reflect the personality and taste of the owner. Each room, whether it be in an old house or a new apartment, an office or an hotel reception area, suggests to me an individual treatment. Good features should be enhanced and bad ones disguised. I believe that interior decoration is the art of accentuating the best and covering up the worst.

☐ Some of the best rooms I know are in such differing environments as 19th century attics, stately homes and 20th century boxes—it's the taste and selection that makes them great.

In the entrance to an Athens apartment I covered the walls with stainless steel panels and formed a pyramidal ceiling separated from the wall panels by a duct for air conditioning. The torso is mounted on black and white marble blocks repeating the floor treatment. The cool, slick look of the metal contrasts interestingly with the white painted, columned vestibule on the left.

In this vestibule I used two antique marble winged lions to support a thick plate-glass top. Simple earthenwear pots containing basil flank a French Empire clock under a Romanesque tombstone dramatically lit by an uplighter.

☐ In the centre of this Athens penthouse hall are a chair and a table copied from the antique by Saridis. In conjunction with Iason Rizos I designed pairs of columns in the naive early 19th century European manner. The deep frieze was the only solution to concealing the air-conditioning ducts. Unlined pure white paper-thin taffeta curtains behind the columns are left undrawn at night to reveal the floodlit rocks adjacent to the building.

Looking from the white columned, black and white marble floored Athens hall through to the long dining room/study/living room, which has a chromium and glass bar table giving a cool, spacious effect.

☐ Looking down the length of the long living room towards the central study area. On the left-hand wall paintings are illuminated with chromium picture lights. The fireplace behind the camera is flanked by a pair of white linen sofas, which, in turn, are flanked by two Louis XVI white-painted cut-velvet covered *fauteuils*. Behind the desk is a bead curtain partly screening the dining area. The entire floor is pure white marble with two vast white textured rugs from Cogolin.

☐ The dining area with a glass-topped dining table with metal frame covered in black leather and highly lacquered Queen Anne style chairs has an antique vase as a centrepiece. The Salvador Dali, which reaches almost from floor to ceiling, dominates the area. The space between the top of the windows and the ceiling is mirrored to enable the curtains to hang from ceiling to floor to give a taller proportion.

Looking towards the Acropolis floodlit. At top left, a portrait of the owner, by Dali, is lit by uplighters. A good example of making the most of the exterior and of the possessions.

□ A collection of 19th century bronze athletes held on cylinders of white marble and the largest on a cube of clear perspex. The curtains are of Thai silk.

On a staircase and landing, my Y-patterned carpet, in red, beige and dark brown, works well with the beige wallcovering and the white marble of the stair balustrade.

☐ A group of aubergine, terracotta and lacquer red 19th century Chinese pottery vases and bowls make an interesting group with a modern ashtray and cigarette box on a glass-topped table.

A group of similar objects linked by origin and by colour, placed on a steel and glass table standing on one of my geometric carpet designs.

One of my octagon design carpets showing how it combines
easily with a striped wall-fabric and curtain material.

Mirrored wall and mirrored alcoves reflect the white tweed-covered wall opposite. The alcoves contain Greek antiquities and books. A Louis XVI *fauteuil*, a steel and glass-topped table, and a chunky armchair covered in coarse linen make an eclectic mixture.

In this study area I designed a desk in chromium and beige leather. Behind the chair a chromium bead curtain transparently divides the study area from the dining area and through it can be seen a fine white-marble Roman torso. To the left of the bead curtain a large palm in a simple earthenwear container is splendidly large in scale.

A small London hallway, with two black horsehair-covered, bright-brass nailed mahogany stools on one of my carpets, has simple elegance.

☐My 'Sammy' carpet in red, banana yellow, dark blue and toffee brown combined with lacquer red walls, banded with wallpaper panels. The asymmetrical arrangement of the miniatures over the chimney gives interest and the chain fireguard is practical as well as decorative.

At Mittagong in New South Wales, I revealed the raw brick walls of the original construction and inserted an 18th century English pine chimney with a fine carving above it. Two sofas in brilliant lacquer red Thai silk vibrate pleasingly with the terracotta coloured bricks.

Inside a Bahamian house, beyond a perspex cube containing a Turkish jewel and a large bowl, can be seen the terrace deck with Molla furniture and a sand dune behind.

A perspex cube holds a stainless steel cylindrical vase with dried Bahamian grass heads and a pottery stag made by my nephew Michael-John Knatchbull. The window is shaded with an opaque white roller blind. There are no curtains in the room but the windows are glazed with smoked glass.

In a house on Eleuthera I put two Bruce Tippetts over two
sofas. This one has a vase of dried grasses to the right of it and
a vast ceiling fan above it,

☐ This room with deep orange walls and a simple modern chimney opening has white plastic-covered furniture, a palm tree, two uplighters and a sculptural object. Basic, elegant and simple.

☐ For a London office, the client had a collection of chessmen, so I devised vitrines to house them. At the far end of the room concealed panels hide a cloakroom, a refrigerator and a bar.

An abundance of 'Peace' roses in a simple Provencal basket reflect the pink of the chintz-covered settee and the cream colour of the cushions.

☐ Old French roses held in a white pottery cylinder are an exciting contrast in colour with the Chinese cockerels and the pink quartz elephants.

For a Long Island home I used a dark brown wall covering and a medium brown tumble twist rug on large tiles of slate. The room depends very much on the dramatic light from a large bay window and to the left can be seen a huge eucalyptus plant which dapples the light filtering into the room.

☐ Rough textured walls are a splendid background for hard edge paintings. This one under the spotlight has added interest by night. The comfortable buttoned sofa is flanked by white opaque perspex cubes and the floor is covered with jute matting.

A table covered in khaki cloth holds a copper funnel with a piece of twisted metal from the Thames and a perspex mounted sculptural object, which are pleasing against raw plaster walls and the slick white plastic doors in this Eleutheran living room.

In my bath/dressing room, my sauna—the smallest in England—has a pine *étagère* and walls, contrasting with the tweed and red lacquer panels.

☐ On a scrubbed wood serving table in a beige painted breakfast room, a bouquet of wildflowers reflects the simplicity and charm of the pottery cream bowl on the right with its stipple decoration.

In a 19th century library, crimson roses reflect the scarlet of the cushion and the bookbindings. Flowers should be coordinated with their background or contrasted with it.

In a New York apartment an interesting arrangement of jade animals standing on clear perspex cubes is underlit by an uplighter, which also gives the plants an exciting translucence. One of my geometric bordered rugs relates well to the pine-panelled room.

☐ A black linen-covered table with a glass top and perspex distance pieces holds a black glazed lamp, a sculpture by Barbara Mortimer and two pieces of *cloisonné*.

My Y-patterned carpet used to cover the walls in this restaurant. I made a screen of duckboarding in cedar wood, lined internally with smoked perspex for the central serving unit. The sliding screens in the recess are teak with red lacquer behind them.

☐ The bar in The Grange restaurant, which was inspired by the chapel at Ryecote, is painted in bronze, khaki and black. The walls and ceiling of the main part of the restaurant are beige and the beams in the foreground are brilliant orange. The raw steel picture frames match the gas-lit chandelier which I designed.

In a Southampton, Long Island, house I used cork wallpaper and under a modern painting placed a tweed-covered sofa and two stainless-steel cubes, one of which holds an ashtray, cigarette box and a plastic object, and the other a vase of full-blown roses.

On an 18th century marble-topped gilt console table I placed an ancient Greek vase next to a galvanised bucket containing dried herbs, flowers and grasses, making a pointful contrast of elements and surfaces.

An arrangement of a lily in a Victorian kitchen jar, lumps of raw glass and a piece of carved rock crystal on a glass-topped aluminium table with an early 19th century portrait dramatically lit from below by an uplighter and from the ceiling by an eyeball spotlight.

An attic staircase in an English country house needed strong treatment, so I covered the walls and ceiling with the same pattern. The roman shade matches the wallpaper and the stairs are covered in simple haircord.

In a London flat in order to give the maximum seating, I made an L-shaped banquette with two opaque white perspex cubes at the ends. Simple, direct and uncluttered, it has sophisticated elegance.

In a New York living room a generous arrangement of furniture gives maximum seating capacity. To the right of the fireplace is a sofa and at right-angles to it a larger sofa is flanked by two chairs.

This chimney, which is late 18th century French marble, is pleasingly balanced by the bookcases to left and right of it and by the armchairs conveniently placed at right angles to the two sofas on either side of the fireplace.

In a 17th century house that I decorated in Holland, dried giant hemlock in a simple lacquered wicker cylinder placed next to a pestle and mortar and two 18th century decoys on a glass and chrome table.

Hosta flowers and leaves work well with this group of
Chinese jade and pottery in a turquoise boudoir.

A number of very dissimilar objects united by a blue theme: lapis lazuli, enamel, pottery, glass and a polarised perspex multiple by Rory McEwen. The yellow water lily in a blue glass vase is related to the yellow and blue sofa cover to the left of the table.

☐ On a glass-topped metal table, against whitewashed walls and a Provençal tiled floor, dried gypsophila and a fresh white lily give a cool, monochromatic look.

□ I used a strong North African design for the ceiling and the walls and painted the beam a plain colour in a typical New York apartment. The fur rug on the bed gives softness in an otherwise disciplined, well-lit room.

In an American apartment, two mirrored screens divide the dining alcove on the left from the sitting room on the right, and a gigantic cactus reflected in one of the panels of the screen produces a sculptural quality.

An entrance hall on Fifth Avenue with a *parquet de Versailles* floor has a mid-18th century, white-painted, marble-topped console table. The painted borders are in bronze and scarlet against panels of cream set on white, inspired by a similar treatment I saw in Jaipur.

Almost all the objects on this table are white and the flowers continue this theme in the white container. The bust of Marie Antoinette was given by the Empress Eugenie to Lady Palmerston.

☐ I designed these nine perspex cubes holding nine cylinders, mounted them under a perspex cube and placed them on a circular table in a pine-panelled library. Dramatic lighting comes from an uplighter on the floor beneath the table.

In a small kitchen in a city block, my 'Celtic' design, used for the roller blind and the wallpaper on the walls and ceiling, gives atmosphere.

In a room with dark maroon walls a scarlet trunk holds a group of white objects. The bare floor is cool for summer.

In a New York apartment I painted the walls khaki and lacquered them. A collection of crystal, shells, minerals, pottery and ivory is effectively displayed and lit in this *étagère* designed by John Mascheroni.

Antique Greek pottery vases and a figure are grouped together under a perspex cube and two of the vases are mounted on clear perspex bases to give varied height.

In the drawing room of a New York apartment I covered the walls in suede leather stitched in panels and framed by silvered wood beading. The Louis XV console with a partly gilded wrought iron base holds a collection of Chinese vases. Mounting the two centre ones on cylinders covered in chamois leather gave added interest to this asymmetrical arrangement.

In a north London house built at the end of the 19th century, demolished walls to provide an open-plan hall/dining room and covered the walls in orange tweed, painted the woodwork white, used dramatic lighting and covered the stairs in my new Y-pattern carpet.

A room on Park Avenue in New York, with four patterns united by colour and texture working against a dark dramatic background, has a stark interesting look.

Modern paintings used in combination with Louis XVI chairs and perspex cubes, uplighters and colour, make this an exciting and dramatic room.

☐ I mounted a painted screen, which was too low for the high proportions of the room, on stainless steel uprights so that the base of the screen was 18″ from the floor, in an apartment on Fifth Avenue. The window is treated with a simple roman shade with a webbing trim. The glass-topped dining table has a bronze metal frame which works well with the black lacquered grey silk covered chairs trimmed with chromium nails. Silver lustre candlesticks hold thin and fat candles, and red lacquer place settings are set with lacquer plates.

☐ This New York apartment entrance hall had too much pine woodwork so I covered the panelling with a rough hessian printed with a white-pigment geometric design of mine but left the doors, architraves, skirting and cornice. The handsome mid-18th century walnut marble-topped table makes a generous and attractive bar. The large arrangement of dogwood in a clear glass vase gives the right scale to the room.

An open-plan area for a suite of desks in an office in New York has stainless steel-clad structural columns and wool covered walls combined with a geometric carpet. It makes an unusual but business like setting.

An office high up in the General Motors building on Fifth Avenue with my brown, black and white geometric design carpet. Lit by downlighters, the red lacquer colour of the upholstery gives warmth.

☐ For a reception area in New York I clad the columns in highly polished stainless steel, covered the walls in tweed and laid one of my geometric carpets wall to wall. Dramatic lighting comes entirely from the ceiling.

An 18th century drawing room in Essex, where I painted the walls palest pink, picked out the cornice in a deeper pink and made the curtains in white chintz bordered in beige and white trimming. The chairs, sofas and cushions complemented the colours in the Pontremoli needlework carpet.

□ Old French roses and peonies, under a Georgian gilt mirror,
on a marble chimney, with Australian minerals and a silver
Mexican egg nestling in a marble snake.

An arrangement of romantic pink roses in a simple white pottery cylinder, next to a red pottery ashtray on a red tweed-covered, glass-topped table.

☐ The entrance hall, staircase and landing of this Swiss house needed a strong, warm design to unite them so I designed this wallpaper, 'Carla', for the area. The motif is white on a caramel ground and the curtains are white linen bound with caramel braid. The doors into the drawing room, in the foreground, are of smoked plate glass.

In a pine-panelled library in Switzerland, I made an alcove covered in toffee-coloured suede and covered the sofa to match. The carpet, which I designed, was made at Cogolin in treacle brown and faded black.

In Yorkshire, a kitchen with a dining alcove seemed to need the warmth of a pine-wood ceiling and with this I used brilliant orange and pink roman shades and a cork floor. The fitments are white and orange.

The curtains and pelmets of a bay window in a house in Derbyshire using my 'Wolfsgarten' design. The window looks on to the conservatory full of luxuriant green flowers, reflecting the greens, pinks and reds of the curtain material.

□ Pale grey flannel curtains trimmed with an inset band of dark anthracite grey flannel, work interestingly with my scarlet and black 'Maltese Cross' carpet.

In the dining room of a country house outside Geneva, I painted the beamed ceiling, the chimney breast, the doors and the windows white. The walls were eggshell lacquered in very dark bronze brown and the room lit by uplighters in each corner and by spotlights from the ceiling. My 'Celtic' patterned carpet covers the floor.

This New York library had existing pine panelling. I painted the interior of the bookcases with white enamel and to lighten the room still more I used one of my geometric rugs, two yellow chairs and a red sofa.

Here objects, paintings and photographs are interspersed with books. Opposite the windows two L-shaped black leather banquettes and two lacquered stools give the maximum amount of seating in this room. A clutter of objects and pictures helps conceal the air conditioning grilles and the hi-fi speakers.

In an apartment in New York's Pierre Hotel, I installed a fine mid-18th century English white and brocatelle marble chimney and on it I placed two Blue-John urns. I covered the walls in stitched panels of suede leather and had the geometric rug specially woven for the room, which is lit by picture lights and uplighters. Antique furniture mixes happily with aluminium and steel glass-topped occasional tables.

☐ An oast house in Sussex, with a circular living room which
suggested that it be tented and that semi-circular banquettes
be made to suit the contours of the room. In brilliant red, scarlet,
apple green and purple stripes, the tent with the banquettes
covered in similar coloured fabric and the apple green carpet
give an exotic look.

Because of the irregularity of a narrow oval staircase in Paris, I decided that the carpet should be a plain colour with a contrasting 4″ width band on either side.

An English country cottage needed a new staircase and I devised these open tread wooden stairs, supported by the wall on one side and by steel uprights on the other, to give a more spacious feeling.

☐ This white and off-white drawing room creates a good foil for a collection of modern paintings and sculpture. Through double doors at the far end of the room is the bronze painted dining room. The cushions on the white sofa are covered with two of my geometric designs.

In a Sussex country house drawing room, I painted the panelling in two shades of beige and white to make a subtle background for a collection of early 20th century English paintings. Two chartreuse green sofas flank the chimney and a third one in coral red faces it. I designed the patterned carpet with a border which follows the contours of the room.

☐ Two Louis XV *fauteuils* are interestingly placed by a modern steel and glass table holding a collection of ivory objects and an oriental lamp with a gathered white poplin shade.

□ This New York living room has a carpet that I designed, suede-covered walls and pure white silk curtains, making a good foil for the collection of pictures, porcelains and other objects.

For a lunch party, four tables are placed together with black and white cloths, in this pool pavilion. The strangely beamed ceiling casts interesting lights.

□ The circular tables covered in black and white geometric cloths are at the four corners of the room when not in use for meals.

For a Swiss country house bedroom, I used a brilliant citrus-yellow fabric for the outside of a tester bed hung from the ceiling with a sharply defined pelmet. The fabric on the walls is the same colour but on a white ground, the sofa is covered in rough white linen and the carpet is cooking-apple green.

In this drawing room the walls and curtains are of a rough textured off-white fabric and the leading edge of the curtains and the trim under the cornice and above the chair rail are two rows of white chevron braid with a narrow band of vermilion between them. The Louis XVI chimney is white marble and the two French chairs provide the only note of colour in this all-white room.

In a suite which I decorated in the Hyde Park Hotel in London, I made a canopied bed fixed to the ceiling in my 'Mint Flower' pattern linen which goes interestingly with my patterned carpet.

For clients in Kent who had a fine Adam chimney, overmantle mirror and elbow chairs, I devised a really country-house drawing room colour scheme, in cream and white paint, quilted pink raw silk, straw coloured linen, shocking pink *faille* and a very pale beige carpet. The patterned curtains reflect all these colours.

☐In a dining room near Maastricht, a modern Dutch painting
of dairy cows is reflected by pottery models on the side table
beneath it. A good example of *cousinage*.

A step ladder provides access to high books in this library in New York. Pottery, photographs, a moth, two oriental tigers and a North African carving meld together in an interesting and personal way.

□ Strangely coloured chrysanthemums relate with the gilded plaster head and the pottery horse, the Louis XV commode and the gilded silver beaker: although unrelated by context, they are by colour and texture.

In the Channel Islands, a remarkable relief sculpture and a fine collection of old masters above the simple stone chimney surround, are hung on plain walls of pale banana yellow. The carpet is patterned in sage greens and faded orange, with the orange sofa and two other sofas in sage green continuing the colour co-ordination.

With Mark Hampton I devised this living room on East 89th Street. My black, white and beige octagon carpet design links the beige walls, the black covered sofa and the white paintwork. Apart from the small lamp to the left of the fireplace, the room is entirely lit with uplighters.

In a New York apartment I used my 'Celtic' design as a rug on the parquet floor, and my large Arabic design wallpaper from Connaissance on the walls and ceiling. The structural concrete beams I painted terracotta and used burnt orange for both the roman shades and the lacquered Parson's table.

In an English country house I converted a ball-room into a games room. The red painted ping-pong table, string matting on the floor, red sofas and aubergine walls, modern lighting and Joe Colombo chairs provide exciting contrast against the Edwardian columns and pilasters.

In Holland, beyond a living room, I devised a small study area with an 18th century wooden chair and table. The walls are covered in brown felt and edged with a red banding which repeats the red of the curtains.

A vitrine with pine architraves lined in brushed steel houses a collection of crystal objects in New York. The geometric bronze coloured cut velvet chair cover in the foreground relates nicely to the wood of the cornice and the architrave.

In the foyer of a Greek apartment, a chandelier taken from an ancient design hangs directly above an ancient Greek vase on a circular table.

☐ In an 18th century white-painted, panelled octagonal room with two alcoves, I placed a circular table with a granite top in the centre and used eastern and European objects.

In a sitting room in the Hyde Park Hotel, I used the same carpet as in the adjoining bedroom and painted the walls white. Gathered fabric lampshades are reminiscent of those in paintings by Vuillard.

A matching pair of red sofas that I designed have cushions in multicoloured pinks and reds, summing up the banding on the leading edge of the curtains and the colours in the carpet. Mary Fox Linton was the associate decorator.

In a double height Paris salon with staircase and gallery, I devised a huge repeat damask linen print in two shades of beige to complement the rough stone chimney, which is flanked by a pair of magnificent Coromandel screens and the two dissimilarly covered sofas. The large window recess is filled by a generous yellow banquette.

Black lacquer Queen Anne style chairs and a glass and metal dining table stand on a Cogolin carpet and the Roman torso is backed by a chromium bead curtain.

In an Athens apartment with a large room divided into a living, a study and a dining area, this view looking towards the fireplace shows four Louis XVI chairs, two sofas and a beige leather-covered desk with a glass top.

At the top of a small town house staircase, the transition between the conventional balustrade and the modern bathroom/dressing room needed an element to fuse the two atmospheres, and the solid balustrade and plate glass screen and door provide it.

In a Bahamian house I devised a very simple beach-like bedroom with raw plastered walls and also made the bedside table in raw plaster with a light under it The bedspread is my 'Tumbling Flower' design and the drawing on the wall is by Denis Wirth-Miller.

☐ With my Swiss associate, Fleur Vulliod, I designed this bathroom. We covered the red painted walls with panels of aluminium-framed mirror to give a greater sense of space. The bath, floor, chest of drawers, dressing table area, washbasin fitment and ceiling are all white.

Four Louis XV polished wood *fauteuils* flank two large sofas on either side of the fireplace in this Fifth Avenue apartment. Looking through the archway, the pine-panelled library beyond repeats the drawing-room cornice and architrave. Four clear perspex tables hold essentials while a pair of leather and oak stools hold books when not in use as additional seating.

In a Paris entrance hall that lacked windows and interest, I made painted panels and used a plain carpet with a plain darker border following the contours of the passage and the hall.

In a dining room in France, panels of late 18th century wallpaper were not large enough to cover all the walls above the chair rail, so I covered the rest of the wall space in marbled paper and treated the dado in the same manner, but with a different marbleised paper. The two fine Louis XVI white marble lions facing the central vase on the chimney piece are dramatically lit against the dark browns, beiges and aubergines of the room.

For a country dining room, I featured the polished wood floor and used one of my octagon design carpets, which looks well with the 18th century dining chairs and the Gothic side table. The painting on the extreme left is by Ivon Hitchens.

A library in a country house needed character, and I decided on an early 19th century gothic feeling. Each section of the bookshelves has a spotlight in order to enhance the bindings.

□ An assortment of photographs, books and personalia makes an interesting and cosy arrangement in this white lacquered bookcase in a pine panelled room.

In a New York apartment, I painted the interior of this bookshelf white enamel to lighten a dark room. Books, porcelain, a picture and jade objects mix happily together.

□ A bar fitment in an English country house library. When closed only the discreet grilles which allow ventilation for the ice-making machine show.

A washbasin under a window with a black granite top. The objects displayed are limited to a large sponge in a glass bowl and a Siamese hand mounted under a perspex cube. The red lacquer base under the washbasin and the drop-forward cupboards above it contain the necessities of a bathroom.

In a Sussex country bedroom, I left the beams as they were and painted the walls white. I used white linen for the beds, the draperies above the headboard and for the dressing table curtains. The carpet, cane chair, table and lamps complete the all-white look. Two early 18th century pieces of dark polished wood combine well with the natural colour of the beams.

☐ High above the East River Drive this drawing room was painted *ecru*. The ebonised floor is a good background for the blue and beige oriental carpet. Beige and bronze colours were continued in the brown sofas, the cushions and the cream wool tweed of the chairs on either side of the French marble fireplace. Gunmetal colour was applied to the pinoleum blinds at the windows to control the quality of light.

For a man's study in America I designed a carpet in beige and brown and used a black and white geometric covering for the sofa and black upholstery for the desk and arm chairs.

In a room in an Eaton Square apartment, I used my 'Turkish Flower' design in toffee and white to cover the walls and for making bedspreads. When the doors are closed they are almost invisible.

In a Geneva dining room I painted the walls aubergine, made scarlet curtains and carpeted it with an aubergine, scarlet and dark blue design. The alcove at the head of the dining table was lined in scarlet box-cloth as a good background to silver, porcelain and other objects.

A London drawing room overlooking Hyde Park carried out in white, off-white and palest sand and beige colours. The textured carpet continues the colour theme and the ebonised floor reflects the colour of the bronze silk velvet tablecloths flanking the sofa opposite the fireplace. Beautifully co-ordinated groups of objects contribute to the comfortable flow of this room.

☐ This office in Brussels has a Louis XVI style *bureau-plat* and apart from the desk lamp, is lit entirely by downlighters. The geometric carpet design reflects the name of the company. White walls, roman shades and upholstery create an immaculate and workmanlike background.

My 'Red Indian' design printed with white pigment on coarse beige cloth, white cotton sofa-covers and Hungarian needle-point weave on two chairs facing the window in this American apartment give a crisp, cool look.

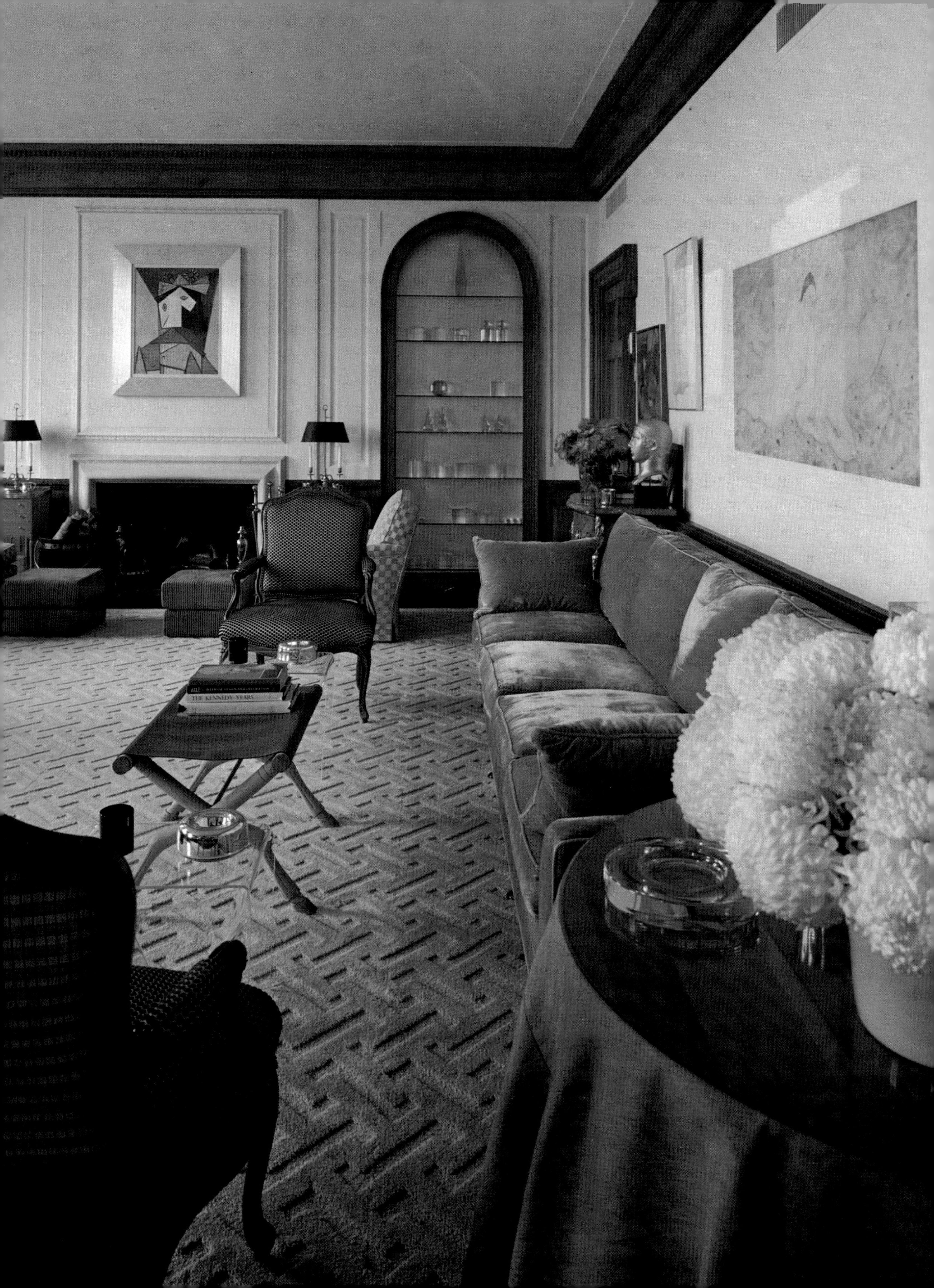
THE KENNEDY YEARS

☐ A large New York apartment drawing room contains a Foujita and a remarkable Picasso. The Foujita is framed in white linen over wood and the Picasso in stainless steel. Two steel alcoves on either side of the fireplace contain a collection of crystal glass objects.

☐ To left and right of a sofa in a Wiltshire country house, two wooden tables have bronze coloured silk velvet covers and each has a piece of lapis lazuli scagliola on which to stand drinks.

☐ The dining section in a small New York living room has a glass table. When not in use it holds a white pottery elephant flower container. The Chinese Chippendale white lacquer chairs have my gothic rose-window print on the seats and in front a pair of mirrored floor-to-ceiling screens reflect other parts of the room and give an added sense of space and depth.

☐ I covered the floor of a 17th century oast house living room with Suffolk rush matting, made a sofa covered in black and beige hessian, another in silver-coloured Thai cotton, used a rustic table of the period with two large candles on it and a pair of metal and glass tables bearing early Turkish pottery. The lighting is mostly provided by uplighters and spotlights.

In an Athens apartment, a tiled washbasin counter holds a triple mirror and outside the window a white canvas sunblind shields the glaring Athenian light. In the distance can be seen the Acropolis.

A bathroom in the Hyde Park Hotel in London designed in association with Mary Fox Linton. Plastic lined curtains over the bath alcove, a Roman shade at the window, a low screen hiding the lavatory and the basin with a beige marble top produce a stylish effect.

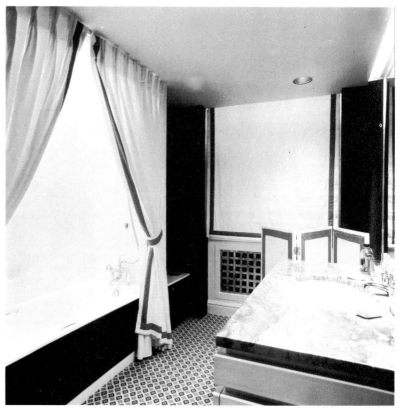

☐ Cupboards in a visitors' room are well disguised because the cornice is returned over the top and the skirting underneath them. The same braided panelling as the other walls furthers the disguise.

☐ My Maltese design carpet in blue and off-white is an easy geometric to use wall-to-wall.

☐ Near the top of the General Motors Building overlooking Central Park, I designed a suite of offices for a British corporation. Stainless steel-clad structural columns and bog brown tweed-covered walls are combined with carpets in brown and off-white. What gives glamour to this corridor in the executives' suite is the simplicity and the dramatic lighting.

An executive office in the General Motors Building, which I designed with my associate, Theodore Triant. Through the windows can be seen the lights on the far side of Central Park. The white tweed curtains continue the theme of my white and brown geometric print on the sofa and chairs. The desk with its glass top and steel base has two oatmeal-coloured, stainless steel-framed chairs facing it.

□ This boudoir painted by Rex Whistler for Brook House in 1937 has a pale blue background and *grisaille* decoration. I continued the late thirties theme by using a boxy sofa and all-white upholstery, and placed early Chinese ceramics on the Louis XVI chimney.

In an Oxfordshire country house a recent Bruce Tippett scroll-top painting dominates the room; it is illuminated, as are the other pictures in the room, by a polished brass picture light. A relaxed room, mixing modern paintings, a chimney piece of 1760, three Louis XVI *bergeres,* comfortable sofas and a strange mixture of objects related by colour, texture or form.

☐ Over a chimney piece in Geneva I placed a large piece of unframed mirror which is exactly the width of the jambs of the chimney. In front of this I put an architectural drawing framed between two pieces of glass, revealing the inscription on the back. Two crystal vases holding marble eggs, and a rectangular vase containing dried grasses create a translucent effect.

☐ A group of ivory objects on perspex cubes, both opaque and transparent, on a large block of wood covered in chamois leather and enclosed by a perspex cover. Putting these objects together gives them an added value which they would not have individually.

☐ For a beach house I made a central kitchen island unit and used black and white geometric glazed tiles. All the units, in white plastic laminate, contrast interestingly with the beige-coloured raw plaster walls.

☐ In a Sussex drawing room, geometric carpeting covers the floor wall-to-wall with a patterned border. The drinks table is aluminium with a granite top.

I mixed an Empire dressing table, an Indo-Portuguese folding chair and an English butler's table in a room with one of my strapwork carpet designs.

☐ A Nassau house, that I architected in association with Robert Stokes, has a feeling of cool airiness with patio furniture of light construction.

In a maze of small rooms I demolished walls and created a kitchen, dining area and beyond it an entrance hall. The stairs can be seen on the left—open treads supported by upright rods of steel.

In a corner of a London drawing room, a conventional 18th century table is brought to life with an arrangement of a number if dissimilar objects united by colour. A Dutch pottery vase holds a generous bunch of dried grasses, herbs and wild flowers. Under a clear and smoked perspex cube, I mounted a shell and a jade vase on a transparent cylinder, giving a cool and edited look.

☐ Wall to wall carpeting in pale ochre and chocolate brown gives sparkle in this small bronze-brown painted living room with a 17th century stone chimney piece. The cornice is late 18th century gothic. A Denis Wirth-Miller painting over the black horsehair-covered mahogany chair contrasts interestingly with the Sandra Blow between the stainless steel obelisks.